Little Books of Guidance
Finding answers to life's big questi

I0661880

THE WAY OF LOVE

Turn

A little
book of
guidance

CHURCH
PUBLISHING
INCORPORATED

This book compiles text from the following sources:
John H. Westerhoff, *Living Faithfully as a Prayer Book People* (Harrisburg, PA: Morehouse, 2004); Carol Anderson with Peter Summers, *Knowing Jesus in Your Life* (Harrisburg, PA: Morehouse, 1993); Mary Gray-Reeves, *Unearthing My Religion: Real Talk about Real Faith* (Harrisburg, PA: Morehouse, 2013); and Vicki K. Black, *Welcome to Anglican Spiritual Traditions* (Harrisburg, PA: Morehouse, 2010).

Church Publishing
19 East 34th Street
New York, NY 10016
www.churchpublishing.org

Cover design by Jennifer Kopec, 2Pug Design
Typeset by Denise Hoff

A record of this book is available from the Library of Congress.

ISBN-13: 978-1-64065-168-5 (pbk.)
ISBN-13: 978-1-64065-169-2 (ebook)

Printed in the United States of America

Contents

Introduction

I pray that you, being rooted and established in love, may have power, together with all the Lord's holy people, to grasp how wide and long and high and deep is the love of Christ, and to know this love that surpasses knowledge—that you may be filled to the measure of all the fullness of God.
—Ephesians 3:17–19, NIV

At the 79th General Convention of the Episcopal Church in July 2018, Presiding Bishop Michael B. Curry called the Church to practice *The Way of Love*. This is an invitation to all of us, young and old alike, to "grow more deeply with Jesus Christ at the center of our lives, so we can bear witness to his way of love in and for the world."

With this call, Bishop Curry named seven practices that can help us grow deeper in our relationship with God, Jesus, and our neighbors as we also learn how to live into our baptismal promises more fully. In today's world of busy schedules, hurried meals, and twenty-four-hour news cycles, it is now more imperative that we make and take the time to center ourselves and follow the way of Jesus. This might mean revisioning and reshaping the pattern and rhythm of our daily life—finding a slice of time to center our thoughts on Jesus. Within these pages you will find ideas to engage in the practice of turn as you walk on *The Way of Love: Practices for a Jesus-Centered Life*.

To be a Christian is to be a seeker. We seek love: to know God's love, to love, and to be loved by others. It also means learning to love ourselves as a child of God. We seek freedom from the many forces that pull us from living as God created us to be: sin, fear, oppression, and division. God desires us to be dignified, whole, and free. We also seek abundant life. This is a life that is overflowing with joy, peace, generosity, and delight. It is a life where there is enough for all because we share with abandon. We seek a life of meaning, giving back to God and living for others and not just for ourselves. Ultimately we seek Jesus. Jesus is the way of love and that has the power to change lives and change the world.

How are we called to practice the Way of Love? Bishop Curry has named seven practices to follow. Like a "Rule of Life" practiced by Christians for almost two thousand years, these are ways that help us live intentionally in our daily life, following our deepest values. These are not add-ons to our day, but ways to recognize God working in us and through us.

Like the disciples, we are called by Jesus to follow the Way of Love. With God's help, we can turn from the powers of sin, hatred, fear, injustice, and oppression toward the way of truth, love, hope, justice, and freedom. In turning, we reorient our lives to Jesus Christ, falling in love again, again, and again. We state "I will, with God's help" as a response to the questions, "Do you turn to Jesus Christ and accept him as your Savior?" and "Will you persevere in resisting evil, and whenever you fall into sin, repent and return to the Lord?" in our Baptismal Covenant. This is what it means to turn to God: pause, listen, and choose to follow Jesus in your daily life.

Practices are challenging and can be difficult to sustain. Even though we might practice "solo" (e.g., prayer), each practice belongs to the community as a whole in which you inhabit as a whole—your family, church, or group of friends. Join with some trustworthy companions with whom to grow into this way of life; sharing and accountability help keep us grounded and steady in our practices.

This series of seven Little Books of Guidance is designed for you to discover how following certain practices can help you follow Jesus more fully in your daily life. You may already keep a spiritual discipline of praying at meals or before bed, regularly reading from the Bible, or engaging in acts of kindness toward others. If so, build upon what we offer here; if not, we offer a way to begin. Select one of the practices that interests you or that is especially important for you at this time. Watch for signs in your daily life pointing you toward a particular practice. Listen for a call from God telling you how to move closer. Anywhere is a good place to start. This is your invitation to commit to the practices of **Turn—Learn—Pray—Worship—Bless—Go—Rest**. There is no rush, each day is a new beginning. Follow Bishop Curry's call to grow in faith "following the loving, liberating, life-giving way of Jesus. His way has the power to change each of our lives and to change this world."

1 ▪ What Does It Mean to Turn?

Like the disciples, we are called by Jesus to follow the Way of Love. With God's help, we can turn from the powers of sin, hatred, fear, injustice, and oppression toward the way of truth, love, hope, justice, and freedom. In turning, we reorient our lives to Jesus Christ, falling in love again, again, and again. How does a person begin to turn to Christ? For Christians, including Episcopalians, it means to remember our baptism.

In the Episcopal Church the rite of Holy Baptism begins with the presentation of adults and older children by their sponsors to receive the sacrament of Baptism in the midst of the worshiping community. Infants and younger children are presented by their sponsors, parents, and godparents, who promise (with God's help) to take responsibility for bringing them up in the Christian faith and life. This represents a promise to participate with them in the life of a community of faith and to practice with them the Christian life of faith. Immediately thereafter follows a series of vows or declarations in the form of three renunciations and three adherences that are foundational to the life of the baptized and indeed a necessary precondition before persons are able to enter into their baptismal covenant with God faithfully. We can think of these renunciations as turning away from something (evil/sin) and towards something (good/love).

A renunciation is an action in which we separate ourselves from a former condition or state by giving up former perceptions and allegiances and accepting the gift of a new set of perceptions and allegiances. To put it in another way, if you are walking in one direction, you see reality from that perspective and act accordingly. But if you repent, that is, turn around and change the direction you are traveling, you see reality from a new perspective and behave accordingly. That is exactly what a person does when he or she makes these three renunciations and adherences.

We first renounce evil, that is, acknowledge evil's influence on our lives and make a formal declaration to refuse, with God's help, to follow, obey, or be influenced by evil. We put our trust in God's help to not be victimized by our experience of evil—evil that, in this case, is the result of its influence on others whose resulting actions affect us. Evil remains a mystery best understood as both an active power or influence that desires to estrange us from God, and the experience of an absence of a God-desired good by the actions of those who have succumbed to evil's influence.

It is important to acknowledge that God does not will evil, but God does permit evil for a greater good. That good is our human free will, a freedom necessary if we are to experience healthy relationships between ourselves and God, between each other, and between ourselves and the rest of God's creation. These relationships are God's greatest desire and good. Evil would have us misuse or abuse this freedom and thereby disrupt or destroy these relationships.

Sins are actions we engage in that are against God's will, but sin is the disposition to act in ways that negatively affect the relationships God intends for us to have with God, ourselves, other persons, and creation. Sin is not so much concerned with determining what is right or wrong as it is with determining what kind of person we will become if we continue to act in some particular way.

The good news of the Christian faith is that God's redeeming power is ever present, making new life possible. However, if that truth is to operate in us, we in our freedom must turn toward God and renounce the power of evil in our lives.

In the Baptismal Rite, we renounce three distinct manifestations of evil: cosmic evil, systemic evil, and personal evil. The first renunciation is this: "Do you renounce Satan and all the spiritual forces of wickedness that rebel against God?" Cosmic evil would have us believe that we have the power to manage nature and history. We experience cosmic evil in the unmanageability of nature and history. We also experience cosmic evil in physical and mental disease and in natural disasters that cause suffering for those who are not responsible for them. We also experience cosmic evil as a consequence of the actions taken by those who believe they can control nature and history.

The second question concerning renunciation is this: "Do you renounce the evil powers of this world that corrupt and destroy the creatures of God?" Systemic evil would have us believe that we have the power to manage human affairs and the social systems we create. We experience systemic evil as the disordering of human affairs in the structures of society and human relationships. Racism, sexism, classism, nationalism, and militarism are all examples. So are the various social, political, and economic systems we create with good intentions, but that result in depriving some person or group of a good that God intends for them.

And the last question concerning renunciation is this: "Do you renounce all sinful desires that draw you from the love of God?" Personal evil would have us believe that we have the power to manage our own lives. We experience the consequences of personal evil when we are influenced by the historic dispositions to sin: pride, envy, nursed anger, sloth, greed, gluttony, and lust, as well as the consequences of our many addictive behaviors, which are themselves expressions of the influence of personal evil.

We are called upon to acknowledge that our lives are unmanageable and that our desire to be independent, self-sufficient, self-disciplined, self-interested, and self-determined, to be effective, to make a difference, to be successful, to be in control—all values of our secular society that are at the heart of our common human sickness and ultimately the foundation for our destruction—need to be renounced.

We turn to God by admitting that we are powerless over those human dispositions that are a consequence of original sin, a doctrine that acknowledges a contradiction between who we really are as God's creation and how in our freedom we choose to live. Although we are formed in the image of love, the image of God, our souls from the moment of birth are affected by other influences that present us with images for our lives that are less than divine, images of human life that would have us deny and distort our total dependence on God and influence us to desire and act as if we have power that belongs to God alone. Or, in the case of some, to believe that they have no control over their lives at all and are always victims of the past or the actions of others.

Having acknowledged our human condition and renounced evil, we turn to three adherences. Having turned away from and rejected one way of life, we make a faithful attachment of our minds, hearts, and wills to an alternative way of life. That is what we mean by an adherence. Our first adherence is to the affirmation that there is a power greater than ourselves who can help us—Jesus Christ. He is the one who can save us, free us, liberate us from the influence of evil and our disposition to sin. To accept Jesus as our savior has a consequence that can be frightening. No longer can we blame our heredity or our environment for our human situation or attribute our behavior to the forces of evil in and around us. We must take responsibility for our lives. And depending on God to aid us, we can know and do the will of God, that is, live a faithful life.

Then, having affirmed Jesus's power to save us, we put our complete trust in God's grace and love—we turn our wills and lives over to God's care. As dependent children, we surrender our lives to God; we allow God to be totally in charge of our lives. We acknowledge that we are not alone; God is present and active in our lives and in history. We need never rely on our own strength and courage, our own wisdom and will. We need not act as if the primary aim for our lives is to be effective or to make a difference. We are to be concerned with being faithful, living in the difference God has already made, and doing God's will, always with God's aid. We do not need to build God's reign; we need only abide in it.

John Westerhoff compares this to floating. Most people, in his experience, are not very good at floating (physically and metaphorically). Perhaps it's true not because floating demands much skill, but because it demands much letting go. The secret to floating is in learning not to do all the things we are prone to do. It is not easy to relax, to give up control, and float.

Typically, when people find themselves tossed from a boat at sea, they respond in one of two ways. Some panic and, being unable to swim, give up and drown. Others attempt to swim to safety. They too drown because they are setting their wills against the water's and the water's always wins. Only those who choose to float can survive. Now floating is not doing nothing. Floating is cooperating with the water. Still, all too few of us are willing to trust the water. Nevertheless, floating is our best analogue for the faithful life. It is neither striving to be in control nor permitting ourselves to be victims who are totally out of control. God calls us to discern what God is trying to do and to cooperate with God.

Having turned our wills and lives over to God's care, we promise to obey Jesus as the one who has legitimate power over our lives and to behave in ways that are a manifestation of Christ's character, that is, to live lives disposed to behave in ways that demonstrate what it means to be in the image and likeness of God. This implies making the character of Jesus the model for our lives and, therefore, apprenticing our lives to Jesus, that is, identifying with Jesus, observing his character or behavioral dispositions, and imitating them.

Think about how you can turn away from the things that separate you from God. What practices help you to turn again and again to Jesus Christ and the Way of Love? How might you use the analogy of floating to put your trust in God's care and abiding love?

2 ■ How Can I Get Started?

Perhaps you have not been able to make a commitment to Christ yet. That is alright. It is important that we come to a relationship with Christ in our own time and in our own way, and anybody who is not able to do that yet should not feel left out of the rest of this book. Ask your questions, sort things out, God will stay with you.

When we turn over our lives to Christ and he begins to give his life to us, things don't always change immediately. In fact it can be a little discouraging when we see some of our "old life" still present. If you look at a tree in the autumn when all the leaves have died, there's nearly always one dry, brown leaf left hanging from a branch and you can't figure out how it manages to stay there. The Christian life is a little like that. We are dead to the old life because Christ has taken it away from us, but there are still dead leaves hanging on, things from the old life that haven't fallen off the tree yet. But it's important to realize that those old leaves are dead. The power of our old way of life to define and destroy us is gone, but that doesn't mean we change completely overnight. Do you yell at bad drivers or snarl at people who cut in line at the supermarket? It's difficult to let these little things go, let alone the big things. In turning to Christ we are open to how Christ defines who we are now. Instead of being bound to the old life, turn it over to him. It's like a leaf hanging on, but it's dead. Let if fall to the ground.

We spend all of our earthly life working out our relationship with Christ. Each day something will crop up and we'll think it's our old ways calling us again. Instead of panicking and seeing the issue as something that will destroy us, we should think of it as something we need to work on. Christ gives us power over the dead leaves which are hanging onto our lives, but we have the responsibility to deal with them as they come up. What we are used to doing is to focus on areas of our own choosing, but the Lord says, "No, this is the area I want to deal with." This can be painful. These are the times when we have to trust the fact that Jesus has transacted something and we have to start acting on it. There are times when we have to act on what we know to be true and then wait for our feelings to follow.

Steam trains have an engine, a coal truck, and a caboose. Very often the engine which is driving our lives is our feelings. Behind it is our faith, being dragged along. But the way in which the Christian life works best is to have the engine be the facts, the givens of the Christian faith; our faith becomes the coal truck feeding the engine; and the caboose becomes our feelings following along behind. The train only really moves when we trust the facts as we hear them and put our faith in them. We need to learn to act on what, in our better moments, we believe to be true. During the most difficult periods, is when God is most active. God is saying, "Are you trusting me when I do not seem to be present?"

Sharing Your Faith

It is important to share your faith. The Reverend Carol Anderson made a very personal commitment to Christ six years after she was ordained. It was a major theological shift for her as well as a personal experience:

> I was going to a seminary to speak, having been invited by one of our bishops to go there. I arrived on the seminary grounds and was horrified to see posters on trees all over

the place saying "Come hear Carol Anderson talk about her conversion!" I was angry and scared! I had shifted gears profoundly in my own life, but the last thing in the world I wanted to be known as was one of those people who go around "witnessing."

Not only was my conversion advertised all over the campus, but when I arrived in the room where I was to speak a large number of the student body was there. At this time I had become well-known in the national church because of the women's ordination controversy, so I had expected more than a handful of listeners, but the trustees were there as well, having cancelled a board meeting to come! There were also a number of bishops. They were all packed into this room waiting for me to talk, and they all had a quizzical look on their faces, as if to say, "What has happened to you?" Picture yourself having somebody set you up to talk about something so utterly personal in front of hundreds of your colleagues. That's the situation I found myself in!

So I faced the crowd and began stammering. I told them I thought I was there to talk about one thing and they wanted to hear me talk about something else, at which point the bishop interrupted me and said, "Tell us what happened to you!" Right out loud! Everyone was straining forward, looking at me, trying to figure out what I was going to say. I started talking very haltingly and obviously didn't say enough because the bishop interrupted again and said, "Tell us what happened to you!" You can imagine how I felt inside! I was so embarrassed. I staggered on as best I could and people began asking me very pointed questions. I finally managed to finish telling the story.

Afterwards people approached me and said, "I don't understand what's happened to you. Is this a change of politics?" They thought I'd become a fundamentalist or some other label they could give me. I fled from the campus to the airplane and back to New York as fast as I could. I would have sat on the plane's wing, if necessary, to get out of there!

By the time the plane landed in New York the anger I felt for the bishop was completely dissipated and I found that something had sprung loose inside of me. I can't tell you what it was, but by the time I was in the terminal building I felt much more comfortable talking about my faith. I went on to talk to other people about these things and found many more were intrigued, too. But it was being forced to put my experience into words which started this whole process of sharing. Even though the situation had been an appalling introduction to telling my story, it had done the trick. It pushed me off home base and got me talking publicly about my faith.[1]

Wherever you are in your faith, it is important to realize that it is not just an emotional transaction but a conscious turning over of one's life to Christ, and it is important to be able to share this with others. That doesn't mean you have to stand on a street corner, buttonhole people and ask, "Are you saved?" You don't have to be a theologian or know all the answers.

A good example can be found in the New Testament—Jesus's

healing of a blind man (John 9:1–34). The religious leaders came to question the man afterwards and asked him what had happened to him, what Jesus had said and done. The blind man replied simply, "I don't know, all I know is that I was blind and now I see." It was his testimony, the truth as he saw it.

In the same way, we can tell people of our experience with Jesus and that God is involved with our lives. We can tell people we believe in Jesus and that something life-changing happened on the cross. We don't have to say much more to anyone than that. You will find something released in you when you begin to do so. The Spirit of God begins to free us up as we learn to articulate our commitment more and more.

Try talking to others about your faith. God will confirm what has happened to you when you begin to share your story. Don't worry about offending people. Don't try to sound like a preacher; just try to be honest about who you are and share it.

Resurrection Life

"Who do you say that I am?" Jesus had asked his disciples during a period of transition in his ministry, after he had spent much time in Galilee teaching about the in-breaking of the Kingdom of God, which is the restoring of a broken and hurting world to a right relationship with God. The disciples answer, "John the Baptist; and others, Elijah" (Mark 8:28). He pressed them: "But who do you say that I am?" Peter replied, "You are the Christ," which to them would mean the Messiah to whom Israel longed for.

Peter had the right answer. Shortly thereafter, when Jesus was arrested, Peter denied that he had ever known him. Peter was absent during much of Jesus's trial and crucifixion. He was off hiding somewhere. Yet after the resurrection, Peter was sought out by Jesus, very personally taken aside by him, and, in one of the most poignant passages in the New Testament, Jesus asks him if he loves him (John 21:15–19). Can you imagine Peter's feelings, hanging his head in shame, afraid to even come into Jesus's presence anymore? Jesus asks him the same question three times and Peter's answers become more and more insistent. "You know that I love you." Jesus gives him back his ministry and says "Feed my sheep, Feed my people."

Throughout the Acts of the Apostles we see Peter taking up leadership in the first church because he really believed that the Jesus who died on the cross was now alive and living in him and in others. And that church grew. On the day of Pentecost three thousand people were added to the church. In the first hundred years after the resurrection of Jesus the church grew to a hundred thousand members. And all that tremendous growth was based on people just like us.

What would happen if we became like those first Christians? The life that Jesus had shown the early church when he was on the earth was now living in them. It's called "resurrection life." What happens when that life begins to work in us?

Power Over Sin in Our Lives

The first thing that resurrection life gives us is power over sin in our lives. It means that the force which drives us to do the things we should not, or do not want to do, is no longer all-powerful. It doesn't mean that we're not tempted. It doesn't mean that we, until the day we die, are not going to get annoyed at the way people cut us off in traffic! But it does mean that we have a power we can call on to help us to stop doing the things we don't want to. Christ will break the power of those things in our lives that go against his way. He has power over sin and he puts that power in us.

Perhaps there is one particular person whom you just can't stand. For many of us there is at least one person who when they walk into a room brings the worst things out in us, instantly. If they open their mouth, we want to say nasty things to them. If they say, "You look wonderful today," we want to reply, "Drop dead!" They push all our buttons at once.

How can we deal with this? What if we prayed that the Lord would really give us the power to love this person. When we arrive at the meeting and see this individual, what if we prayed, "Lord, give me the power to deal with this." Listen for the little voice in your conscience telling you, "If you act lovingly toward them I will give you the power to follow through."

That is how God operates in our lives; God awakens our conscience and points us towards what is right. We become increasingly fine-tuned to the ways of God. God will give us the power to triumph over these problems but we have to take the first step. Once we do, God will come right along with us. Sometimes we say, "Lord, take this away from me," and nothing happens. We wonder what God's up to and what's taking so long, but what God is really saying to us is, "If you desire to be my follower and you know what is right to do, start acting on it in obedience and my Spirit will come and help you with it." What God wants to see is the intention of our hearts. Once we move in the right direction he will be there with us.

That is what it means to have power over sin. When we are left to our own devices we have only ourselves to rely on, but in the Christian life God gives us power to draw on. God keeps working with us on our problems. It's not, "Lord come and take this away from me," nor is it us trying to make it on our own, it's a combination of the two. We know what we are supposed to do, we step out and God helps us fulfil it. We then begin to experience what resurrection life is all about.

That is what happened to the early disciples. They started to do the things they'd seen Jesus doing when he was walking with them on earth. Who in the world would call Peter to be their spiritual leader? But look what happened to him. Jesus built his entire Church upon Peter's leadership. If Jesus can do that with Peter, there's nothing he can't do with any of us! That is what is so exciting about resurrection life! It is a life with power over sin.

Death, Where Is Thy Victory?

The second thing that happens in resurrection life is that death no longer has any grip on us. Death, that sense of things always falling apart, is a byproduct of a world out of relationship with God. Remember that God said if Adam and Eve ate of the tree of the knowledge of good and evil they would perish (Genesis 3:1–24)? Spiritual death is reversed in Christ. Not only did he break the power of death when he was raised from the dead, but he also broke the fear of dying in us. We can actually become people who are hopeful—hopeful in situations where the world would think no hope is possible. Even if we physically die, it is not the end of our life, we live in Christ forever.

If you've ever been to the funeral of someone who really was a committed Christian, you'll have noticed an enormous amount of joy in the service. Of course, there is sadness; people cry because they're going to miss somebody; but the hymns are hymns of joy and gladness, of resurrection and hope, just about the most exciting texts imaginable. That type of funeral is such a celebration it is almost a party. Even though the family knows a person has physically died and misses him or her deeply, they know that their loved one is living in the presence of God.

When we live in the resurrection, death does not have the power to hold us anymore, either ultimately or in the daily business of living. The secret is to find a calm center in the midst of the "death" that hits us day to day. Sometimes we ask God to change the situation, but what God does instead is to change us in the situation, rather than change the circumstances.

There is a story of a man in which one of his sons had been brain-damaged in a car accident, another son had committed suicide at junior college three months later, and he and his wife had not recovered from these shocks. After sharing his story, he said, "You know, the strangest thing is that I feel my faith has strengthened more than ever before. Not that I don't get depressed at times. I went to a psychiatrist because I couldn't deal with my family's grief, let alone my own. Yet something has been released in me that makes my faith more real today that it ever was before. It hasn't given me my son back, and it hasn't healed my other boy, but I have come to know a power I would never have experienced otherwise. Despite this tragedy, I really feel that death has no power over me."[2]

There is a power in the death and resurrection of Jesus which tells us that, although death still is strong in the world, Christ will give us his resurrection life; and that, if we draw upon him, we will have joy even if everything else falls apart. As we grow day by day and week by week in relation to Christ, we discover that there are situations in life which are seemingly random and meaningless, but in the midst of which we will, nevertheless, have joy.

God will give us the power that we need to do difficult and risky things. Why do Christians move into the difficult areas of the world for social welfare? Or work with the poor in Calcutta? Who, historically, are the ones who started hospitals, improved prisons, ended slavery? More Christians have died for their faith and commitment in the past century than in all other previous centuries! Resurrection life is life lived without fear of death. Resurrection life is rejoicing in new life.

Satan Is Conquered

Satan is that personal spiritual force at work in the universe opposing the things of God. Some believe in him, some don't. Jesus believed in him; Satan was the one who thought he could destroy Jesus by having him put to death. When Jesus was resurrected from death, Satan's power to undo and destroy things in this world was no longer total. This does not mean he cannot still hurt people's lives. Satan often whispers in our ears, "You don't really believe all this about Jesus do you? You don't really think you're going to change?" But, when we belong to Christ, that evil power in the universe does not have ultimate sway over us. There are people who have been destroyed by drugs and the hellish life of degradation that goes along with that, people who have seemed hopeless, yet have been transformed by the power of Jesus. Satan's grip has been broken.

What Does This Mean in Everyday Life?

One of the first things that happens when we commit our lives to Christ is that we realize we are defined by what he says about us, not by what we say about ourselves or by what the world says. We need to know what that means.

When we look in the mirror in the morning how do we feel? When we are really depressed, what do we think about ourselves? How do we describe ourselves in those moments? We don't always like what we see.

What does Christ say about us? He says we are a beloved daughter, a beloved son, a beloved child. He says we are adopted into his family and have been given the rights to everything he has. He says that he died for us. If we were the only ones in the universe who needed saving, he would still have died for us. We are the wonder of God's creation, the joy of his life. Jesus sees in us something extraordinary.

Jesus calls us into his new life by loving us. Jesus sees what we can be. This is a whole new way of building our self-esteem, not by saying to ourselves, "I am wonderful," but by his loving us the way we are. "Beloved child in whom I am well pleased"—that's what he says about us. That is what God said to Jesus at the time of his baptism.

One of the stories that best illustrates this is from the play *Bus Stop*. One of the characters, Cherry, has had a pretty seedy, turbulent life, and a guy named Beau falls in love with her. She is petrified that Beau will find out about her past, so she tells him that she's lived a very bad life and that she's not worthy of him. Beau responds by saying, "I love you the way you are. I don't care how you got that way."

God says that Christ has given himself for us and that we are cherished because of that. God will love us as we are, and that brings us the freedom to start acting the way we should, to become the kind of person God sees in us. Christ starts working in our souls and gives us his love. He restores the image of God in us that has become blurred by our living apart from him, then we begin to become like him.

Many of us grow up in families where, unintentionally, we are not told we are loved. Much is expected of us, but there is little overt sense of our worth expressed. These feelings of inferiority begin to stick to our insides and we never quite believe that we are accepted. But Christ says, not only are we accepted, but we are also cherished. Our self-esteem begins to be repaired, and we start to feel loved.

The Power to Forgive

We hang onto a lot of hurt in our lives. There are moments when God will tell us quite clearly to let go of it.

The life we have in Christ is an adventure that will not be simple, easy, or dull. It will take us in all kinds of directions. We will be doing things we never thought we would do, saying things we never thought we would say. Being a Christian—a disciple, a follower of Christ—is not a panacea which creates immediate happiness. Any religion that claims that it makes life perfect is selling us a cheap bill of goods. But when Christ comes to live in us, we will have a life we would not want to trade, even when the tough times come along. Christ gives us a quality of relationship with God we will never have experienced before. The adventures we will have in prayer, in study of Scripture, in witness and in life itself will, day by day, show us the reality of God's power and his love.

How do we sum up the Christian life? Karl Barth (a theologian who died in 1968) was interviewed in *Time* magazine in which he was asked to sum up his theology. In response he began to sing the children's hymn, "Jesus loves me, this I know, for the Bible tells me so."

Your faith has to start there, in a recognition that God loves us. God loves all of us. There are no exceptions. No matter what our past is, no matter what others may say, this is the fundamental witness of the Christian faith. God loves us and in order to win us back to himself, in Christ went to the cross and was raised from the dead to be able to live in us and through us, so that we might be witnesses to his life in a world that is caught in the jaws of death. Behind all of the complexities and under the surface there is a world longing to hear that Jesus loves us. That is the great joy about witnessing to the Christian faith.

3 ▪ How Do I Practice Following Jesus?

The process of faith is a relational adventure. In the beginning of a spiritual quest, we tend to be motivated by a desire to feel better and to have a stronger sense of direction for life. But as spiritual truths begin to make a positive difference, you may consider a certain commitment to the author of those truths. We can isolate the teachings of Jesus, but they are tethered to the person of Jesus. They emerge from him. For Christians, this means they come from God. Christians have faith, then, not only in the words and teachings of Jesus, which have proven true and trustworthy, but in Jesus himself. To begin to know Jesus both by reading about him and through the experience of grace is to know God.

Just as faith is relational, God is relational. Christians speak of God as "Trinity," expressed in traditional language as Father, Son, and Holy Spirit. This means God is the Father and origin of all creation (Creator); God is the Son, Jesus, who connects humanity to the fullness of God (Redeemer); and God is the Holy Spirit, the sustainer who offers wisdom and guidance to hold us in grace (Sanctifier). Each one's identity and being is energized by the relationship of love and grace that the three share. One does not exist without the other. Their relationship makes them who they are distinctly, and at the same time, they are completely one.

Followers of Jesus come into relationship with this Trinity, the fullness of God, through relationship with Jesus. As the persons of the Trinity derive their identity from their relationship with one another, Christians derive our identity from life with God in Jesus Christ. As the Trinity shares divine love and grace with followers of Jesus, we go forth to share the same with the world. This is how God relates intimately within God-self and with all humanity. As I trust this relationship and the overall relationality of God, I find that my faith in God only grows.

What's in a Name?

Christians often speak of belief or faith in Jesus Christ. "Christ" is not Jesus's last name but instead a title. It refers to his calling as Messiah, the anointed one, who would be savior to the Jewish people. This concept comes with a long history, but it is enough here to say the idea that people needed a savior to save them from themselves, to overcome the grave injustices of the world and defeat evil, was fairly widespread in the first century. It still is with Jews and Christians, although we understand it in different ways. Jews await the first coming of the Messiah and believe that salvation is not for later, but something to work for now. Christians believe Jesus is the Messiah, but also work to bring about God's kingdom now and hope that Christ will come again to reorder the creation according to God's will and purpose.

Christians refer to Christ particularly when we are describing spiritual encounters with grace, which can be mystical, mysterious, or even miraculous. It is a way of highlighting the divine nature he embodies eternally. The more deeply we commit to these truths at the heart of our own lives, and seek to be rooted in his graceful way, the more we develop our "life in Christ."

Followers of Jesus who wish to experience the intimacy of this dynamic relationship and develop a conscious understanding of the Christian framework, eventually engage the spiritual practice of *commitment*.

The Spiritual Practice of Commitment

Like any practice, a spiritual practice builds our capacity for something. The spiritual practice of commitment builds our trust in Jesus's teachings, and in turn, Jesus himself. It takes us beyond intellectual belief, and into a relationship with the relational God, walking together on God's graceful way.

Allow yourself to imagine a relationship with God. Imagine that God loves you unconditionally, and imagine returning that love for God. If you do not feel it, simply pray for the capacity to love God as much as God loves you. Imagine that for today, you could commit to this relationship with the God of grace, even though life is not perfect.

When we deepen commitment, sometimes we must clean up loose ends. Do you need to forgive God for letting you down or not giving you something you asked for? Imagine forgiving God.

You may leave God tomorrow if you wish, or you may choose to continue loving God tomorrow. Sit with the possibility—the freedom—of both for a minute. Imagine loving God *today* as much as God loves you. Make it a practice that you take up one day at a time.

Making Commitments

It may feel odd to commit to unseen things, but it is something we do throughout our lives. We commit to our families, marriages, and partnerships. We commit to friendships, jobs, physical self-care, study. We dedicate time and energy to all sorts of people and enterprises. These are seen realities, but unseen realities motivate them. We commit to our relationships because we love the people with whom we have them. We cannot literally see this love, but we know it is there.

When we practice commitment, it is for the sake of that love, that bond, and the desire to deepen it.

In a marriage two people practice commitment daily. They intertwine with one another through good times and bad, highs and lows, misunderstanding and new understanding. They can have faith in the unseen gifts of God, such as love, in the midst of difficulty. Long-term couples look back and see the fruits of their practice of commitment, where at the time, they weren't sure they would make it to the next day.

A practice of commitment to a spiritual relationship with God is like that. It is an eternal union capable of surviving all circumstances of life, including physical death. Theological belief systems may shift, but faith built on loving relationship is solid. It often defies logic. Just like the ups and downs that are part of loving relationships, in the same way we can place our confidence in our relationship with God, even when sometimes there is no good reason to believe in God. Look at the world—there are so many reasons not to believe in God. Yet when we are conscious of God, we can believe in and commit to God. When we are conscious of the love of God, we can commit to loving God as God loves us.

As with the practices of *noticing* and *grace*, *commitment* to being conscious of the unseen love of God teaches us that when we think there is nothing there, there is more than we could have imagined. Remember the words from Hebrews: "Now faith is the assurance of things hoped for, the conviction of things not seen" (11:1). In the stories of the Gospels, those who followed Jesus sometimes did not understand where he was going or what he was doing—disciples constantly asked, "Where are you going?" "Where are we going?" "What are we doing?"—but they committed to following. Conscious of God's presence through Jesus, his followers exercised the spiritual practice of commitment to move more deeply into their life with him, even when they weren't sure about the details. And they took it one day at a time.

People struggle to believe in the resurrection of Jesus from the dead because it is physically impossible. Still, it serves as a paradigm story for Christians, not because it is provable or in need of defense, but because it speaks something of the essence of God. The resurrection reflects God's promise to keep coming back to be in relationship with humanity, even in the face of rejection. God committed to loving people one more day. This is grace: showing up against all odds, loving us when we least expect or deserve it. If we have experienced this grace, then the resurrection of Jesus might make sense. Could you have faith in God, if God has this much faith in you?

Commitment builds on the trust we develop as we grow conscious of grace. This happens little by little over the course of the relationship. It might seem a small thing. But as we have seen with the mustard seed, small things can grow very large.

Heresy Guaranteed

Some Christians are concerned about believing the right thing. We humans often want our intellectual ducks in a row. We want to organize life, even eternal life, even though that enterprise makes about as much sense as trying to nail Jell-O to a tree. God is always good for a surprise, coloring outside the lines, and jumping out of the boxes into which we have placed God.

Nonetheless, working through our language is part of making faith real. Eventually, those conversations result in something we call doctrine, or authorized statements about faith. Christians have doctrine, as do most religious groups. Our doctrine comes from the ordering of faith conversations from early Christianity. It is different than being conscious of the presence of God, but both are part of the root system of faith.

Christians engage the doctrines of our tradition as they were handed down through the years, and expressed in the earliest creeds and formulations of the faith. Those who practice commitment are bound to think about God, theology, and the world. Sometimes our conclusions will match those creeds, and sometimes they will not. If this sounds like heresy, it is. Committed Christians commit heresy regularly. We can't help it. It is part of an active spiritual life to consider and wrestle with the history, formulas, and words that shape faith.

A growing proportion of Americans are "spiritual but not religious." That is, they are interested in a personal experience of spirituality and even faith, but not necessarily religious practice or doctrine. They think being religious and faithful means agreeing with all the faith statements. Some of them go to church. They may even recite the creeds, but they do not necessarily believe everything they say. They may believe in the spiritual truth that God always comes back into relationship with humanity, but they do not buy the historical bodily resurrection of Jesus. Followers, people conscious of the *presence of* Jesus, are not necessarily committed to the theological *statements about* Jesus.

The earliest followers of Jesus, who also lived in a period of rapid cultural and intellectual change, had no hard and fast creeds. They had a living experience, which grew into a growing body of trust. They lived lives that witnessed to the power of Jesus's life, death, resurrection, and teachings. Followers, not doctrine, reflected faith through the spiritual practice of commitment to the graceful way of Jesus.

It is possible to substantiate this through physical evidence. Holy sites in Israel, where Jesus is believed to have lived, taught, been on trial, been convicted, died, and appeared in the resurrection, offer archeological evidence to support the presence not only of Jesus, but of the generation of followers who have witnessed to his life, death, and resurrection.

But don't take their word for it. Know it for yourself through conscious experience. We cannot believe only what others tell us, or what ancient (and still valuable) faith formulations ask us to recite. We must experience them as real for ourselves.

In this postmodern world, especially give the death of institution Christianity as it has been known for the last few hundred years, we may feel we cannot trust the institution of the church. Everyone has to reach a personal understanding of such words as "truth," "belief," "faith," "God," "resurrection," and more. There is much more fluidity between doctrinal adherence and spiritual experience. This is to be expected. It is part and parcel of life today.

Yet those who continue to follow Jesus have faith and practice commitment to walking the graceful way, trusting in the core truths he taught and lived—one day at a time. The story of the resurrection says Jesus was not recognizable after he rose from the dead. Long-time Christians should not, therefore, look for that which we have always seen, but for the tiny new thing taking root that may at first seem unrecognizable. Following Jesus and his graceful way, we cannot go wrong.

Return to the Spiritual Practice of Commitment

Imagine that you love God as unconditionally as God loves you. Pray that you might have the capacity to love God as God loves you. Could you forgive God for letting you down or not giving you something you asked for? Imagine that for today, you could commit to this relationship with the God of grace, even though the relationship is not perfect and neither are you. Companion with the God of grace just for today.

4 ▪ What Can I Do to Go Deeper?

We may understand baptism as a call to a deeper faith, "a divine summons to stand forth from the casually believing crowd" that we hear days, months, or even years after the day the water was actually poured over our heads. This call may be heard at a time of spiritual crisis when matters of faith take on an imperative they have not had before, or simply in a time of awakening to faith in the course of searching for meaning in one's daily life. But however and whenever it is heard, the call of baptism is not just to an affirmation of faith; it is also a commissioning for ministry that might be called an "ordination of the laity." Baptism not only provides strength for the spiritual struggle throughout one's life, it also brings us into the communion of Christ's church: it "sets one within the people of God, the holy priesthood; it brings one into the eucharistic fellowship."[3] These are the enduring commitments of baptism at any age, and we will spend a lifetime entering into the mystery of living them fully and completely in our daily lives.

We learn the significance of our baptism only by practicing the faith into which the baptismal rite initiates us, and the questions of the Baptismal Covenant in the prayer book can provide a helpful framework for that practice, as we seek to live out our commitment to the Christian faith and life. The five questions of the Baptismal Covenant in the 1979 Book of Common Prayer are an expansion and interpretation in modern language and sensibilities of a question that was added to the baptismal rite of the 1662 prayer book by Robert Sanderson, later bishop of Lincoln, during a time when its use was forbidden by the government. The question followed the renunciations of evil and the affirmation of faith, and asked: "Wilt thou then obediently keep God's holy will and commandments, and walk in the same all the days of thy life?"

The five questions of the Baptismal Covenant explore the five areas of Christian living, revealing the landscape in which faith unfolds. First, Christians live in community, even when they experience physical solitude. This community life involves teaching and learning, sharing in the bread and wine of Christ's body, and praying for others, for the church, for the world, for one's own salvation and wholeness.

Second, Christians develop the discernment to recognize evil and the courage to resist it. They learn to see and "name" all that draws them away from God, and when they fall into sin, they choose to repent and return to the Lord. This awareness of the need for ongoing conversion has been expressed in terms of sanctification, especially through the sacraments, and growth in a life of holiness through daily prayer. This is what it means to turn to Christ.

Third, Christians offer witness to the Good News by both word and example. The study of Scripture and the practice of faith are inseparable in the Episcopal Church, which has a rich tradition of learning and literature that yearns to be shared with others.

Fourth, Christians live a life of service, seeking and serving Christ in all persons. This service is offered in a multitude of ways, from the church's ministries of pastoral care and outreach to the daily care of others practiced by individual Christians in the home, workplace, and marketplace. The Benedictine tradition is of particular influence in its emphasis on hospitality and the structuring of a communal life that benefits all.

And fifth, the Christian life involves a commitment to work for justice and peace among all people, and thereby to respect the dignity of every person. For Episcopalians this call to justice and peace has taken many forms, including efforts to abolish slavery, to provide a more just and equitable distribution of the world's economic wealth, and to uphold the equal human rights of all people.

Learning Repentance

In asking us to "persevere in resisting evil," the second question of the Baptismal Covenant calls us to the hard but hopeful work of nurturing spiritual growth and knowledge of God in a world that continually challenges the development of such virtues as goodness and love, justice and peace. If our baptism is the place where we start our journey, our sanctification and growth in holiness will "have to be worked out with long-term and dogged perseverance."[4] Our commitment is renewed and tested and worked out in the private and public spheres, in our prayers offered in secret and in the daily decisions and acts that shape our lives. In this process of persevering day by day to overcome the forces that pull us away from the life of God, we rise and fall time and time again. As John McQuiston points out in the title of his modern paraphrase of the sixth-century Rule of St. Benedict, in a life of ongoing conversion "always we begin again." Such an awareness of the need to begin again throughout our lives dispels any mirage of easy upward mobility in the spiritual life, but also gives us strength and courage to persevere in hope, until Christ is indeed the center of our whole life.

This second question echoes the threefold commitment made earlier in the rite by baptismal candidates to "renounce Satan and all the spiritual forces of wickedness that rebel against God." In the early church such renunciations were expressed both verbally and physically, as the candidates turned their whole bodies to face the west, where they believed the devil was symbolically to be found. In some liturgies they were directed to "breathe on him so that you may begin the battle against him." After they spoke the words of renunciation, they then turned to the east, the place of light, and allied themselves to Christ. This process was repeated three times, with the candidates renouncing every aspect of their former life that contradicted their new life in Christ, and adhering to a new Lord and Savior.[5] In this way the spoken renunciation of evil and repeated turning toward the light reflected the inward and spiritual process of what it meant to leave paganism behind and enter the Christian community.

The fourth-century bishop Theodore of Mopsuestia described the renunciations in his instructions to the candidates for baptism in his diocese, telling them that the meaning intended by the affirmation "I renounce Satan" is that "we have nothing in common with him." Through the grace of Christ we are freed from oppression and liberated from slavery. "Now I know my benefactor," we are able to affirm. "I recognize my Savior. For truly my benefactor is my Savior, who created me when I was not, who grants me favors every day, who does not turn away from me even when I rebel." And so in our baptismal renunciation we pledge to avoid the company of Satan, vowing never to seek it again. "I shall have nothing to do with him," we resolve, "for he was the cause of evils without number." This, Theodore concludes, "is the meaning of 'I renounce.'"[6]

For some early Christians this profession of faith would mean a change in their work or professional life; teachers, for example, were often required to instruct pupils about the Roman gods and religious beliefs, while government officials were expected to be loyal to the various cults of worship. Those Christians who refused to worship the Roman gods or the emperor as required by law lost their jobs—or even their lives, martyred at the hands of Roman authorities. Renunciations of paganism were not made lightly. And the cost of discipleship has remained high in times throughout history and to our own day in those places where the political powers are bent on destroying those who affirm their belief in Christ alone. Countless Anglicans (including Episcopalians that are part of that heritage) over the centuries have given their lives over to death rather than compromise their faith in Christ, from the English reformers of the sixteenth century to bishops James Hannington and Janani Luwum in Uganda to civil rights worker Jonathan Daniels during the Civil Rights movement in the United States.

Like the modifying of renunciations in the baptismal liturgy, now spoken rather than acted, this experience of turning from one way of life and entering another is less tangible for many Episcopalians today. Many of us grew up in households that practiced some form of Christian faith, so our experience of conversion may be more of an ongoing deepening and discovery of adult faith than a watershed moment of clear and unwavering commitment. And yet one of the most beloved and sustaining dimensions of the Episcopal way is its affirmation of the holiness of ordinary life, and the opportunities to love God afforded by the present moment, in whatever circumstances we find ourselves.

Practicing Holiness

Growth in holiness, like physical development, does not just happen; it must be nurtured and tended with intention and care. For most of us, that nurture takes place in community, among those with whom we live and work and worship. When Benedict of Nursia advised his monks how to resist the "zeal of bitterness which separates from God" and to foster the "good zeal which separates from evil and leads to God," he immediately placed that struggle in the context of community life:

> This, then, is the good zeal which members must foster with fervent love: "They should each try to be the first to show respect to the other" (Rom. 12:10), supporting with the greatest patience one another's weaknesses of body or behavior, and earnestly competing in obedience to one another. No monastics are to pursue what they judge better for themselves, but instead, what they judge better for someone else.[7]

In other words, holiness is not learned in isolation but in community, not in abstract theological principles but in showing patience and care for others, and in paying attention. In the words of Joan Chittister, holiness is learned by "caring for the people you live with and loving the people you don't and loving God more than yourself"; we must develop eyes to see and ears to hear, "listening for the voice of God everywhere in life, especially in one another" and here in the present moment.[8]

This aspect of "listening for the voice of God everywhere in life" on the path to holiness has been practiced in myriad ways through the centuries, but one strong characteristic of spirituality is its focus on the simple, ordinary, "daily" quality of human life lived in the presence and companionship of God, in the fellowship and community of others. We see this focus in the short prayers and blessings that punctuated the days and nights of Celtic Christians in the early centuries of the church in Britain. "I kindle my fire this morning, in the presence of the holy angels of heaven," a mother would pray at the lighting of the morning fire. "God kindle Thou in my heart within, a flame of love to my neighbor." Whether tending fields or herding sheep, walking to town or another place of work, a journey blessing would always be said, recognizing the presence of the One who accompanied them on the path:

I on Thy path O God

Thou God in my steps.

Bless to me, O God

The earth beneath my foot,

Bless to me, O God,

The Path whereon I go.

And when the day's work was done, a bed-blessing would bespeak the security of the encompassing God:

I lay me down with Thee, O Jesus

And mayest Thou be about my bed,

The oil of Christ be upon my soul,

The Apostles' Creed be above my head.

O Father who wrought me

O Son who bought me

O Spirit who sought me

Let me be Thine.

Like the Anglican spirituality that evolved from it, the Celtic world was deeply incarnational, the place in which God revealed himself. "Birth and death, waking and sleeping, and in between all the working hours of each day," writes Esther de Waal, "are all part of a life in which the presence of God is known. Living and praying are inseparable."[9]

That is why one spiritual practice many Episcopalians find helpful in their efforts to live a more centered and ordered life in today's fragmented and chaotic culture is the tradition, learned from Benedict, of establishing a rule of life as a framework and guide for spiritual growth. In her book subtitled *A Rule of Life for the Rest of Us*, spiritual director Margaret Guenther notes that "a good rule is not a complicated 'how-to' manual, but a sheltering and sustaining *place*. A refuge—not for hiding or avoidance, but for gathering strength." Thus a rule of life is not a list of things to do, like a recipe or an instruction manual, but a framework, a trellis, a structure, a secure and steady place in which our spiritual lives find the nourishment they need to deepen their life in God and to grow in wisdom and wholeness. While there are many different ways of developing a rule of life, with a wealth of riches from which to learn in the church's tradition, a rule should be grounded in real life, practical and useful in the here and now. "Making a rule," Guenther reminds us, "must have something to do with real people trying to get through their days mindfully and fruitfully."[10]

A rule of life can be simple or elaborate, and tends to evolve and adapt over time as one's life circumstances and spiritual needs change. Time set aside monthly or yearly for solitary retreat and rest is often one aspect of a rule, and some people choose to include particular acts of service to others or opportunities for pilgrimage. Regular meetings with a confessor or spiritual director can be an important part of a rule, especially now that the practice of private confession has been lost in many parts of the Episcopal Church. While the General Confession may help us to acknowledge the human failings we share with others and our corporate guilt for societal injustice, there are times in our lives when spiritual growth is hindered by a deep-seated wound or persistent habit that can only be healed and brought to light through particular and specific conversation with a wise companion. The Celtic church in particular cherished the art of *anamchairdeas* or soul-friendship, with several of their early monastic rules addressing the duties of these spiritual guides, and in recent decades the art and practice of spiritual direction has seen a revival in the Episcopal Church.[11]

Thus rules of life may vary widely in their scope and complexity, but daily prayer of some form is an essential part of any rule. Many use the various rites for morning and evening prayers or Compline from the prayer book; others incorporate meditation or contemplation, praying with beads or the labyrinth, into their daily routine. Most include the psalms or other passages from Scripture, and readings from books on spirituality, both classic and modern.

With the wealth of resources available today, it can be difficult to know where and how to begin, so a consideration of the ways Christians who have gone before us have practiced a life of ordered daily prayer is a useful guide.

Living in the Presence

Whether through praying the offices throughout the day and night in a "cascade of prayer" shared with countless others or offering family blessings on our daily work and journeys, Episcopalians take seriously the need to live in awareness of the presence of God and thus to "pray without ceasing." Many place a high value on the ordering of their days, their work and family life, their relationships with others, and their prayer and worship so as to allow the process of sanctification to proceed unhindered by the distractions of wasted time and busyness that lead only to fatigue and confusion. Most see their participation in the Sunday Eucharist as an important part of their worship of God, and have some form of regular daily spiritual practice that includes prayer, silence, and reading. To that end, they often design and stick to an informal rule of life to help guide them along the way.

The ways that Episcopalians have sought to live out the baptismal call of continual and ongoing conversion, of living more and more the new and abundant life of which Jesus spoke, vary so considerably they may almost seem too dissimilar to be of the same tradition. But it is important to keep in mind that the Anglican Church was formed as a distinctive "church of the middle way" at the Reformation, one in which Catholic and Protestant sensibilities struggled to coexist side by side. Over time those of Puritan and High Church, Evangelical and Anglo-Catholic, liberal and conservative persuasions have all had a place at the table—and at our best moments, with generosity and grace.

The willingness to live at peace with differences of practice and theology and to have a healthy humility about dictating the religious convictions of others is a hard-won characteristic of the Episcopal Church's Anglicanism that may be especially instructive in today's conflicted world. We need to pay attention to how this willingness gave our ancestors "a way of talking about God and about the Christian life that was not confined to those who shared their particular theological concerns within the controversies of their day." This conversation could take place then—and perhaps would be made less acrimonious today—by the practice of doing "theology less by the systematic examining of doctrinal structures than by reflecting on the shape of Christian life."[12]

Yet this integration of theology and spiritual practice should not be misinterpreted as a lack of concern for doctrine—which is a common yet mistaken impression often held by those who see the Episcopal Church as "soft" on theology or "wishy-washy" in what it believes. Core beliefs and doctrines do inform and shape both our prayer and our practice of the Christian life, as we "continue in the apostles' teaching and fellowship, the breaking of bread and the prayers" while also being attentive to the need for continual repentance, returning, and renewal in our daily lives. For many who have gone before us, theology—thinking about God—could never be separated from sanctification—seeking after God while living a life of personal holiness. And if we could begin our conversations today with the common language of living holy lives, rather than focusing on statements of doctrine, we might learn much-needed tolerance and humility in our debates, recognizing that those with whom we disagree aspire to the same holiness of life that we do.

5 ■ How Do I Live a Life in Christ?

Living a holy life, according to Jeremy Taylor, a seventeenth-century theologian, requires that we devote our lives to the right end, namely, to grow into an ever-deepening and loving relationship with God. We must also live for others, all others, including those who will be born long after we have died. Another way to put it is that we must live a righteous life, a life committed to a right relationship with God, self, all others, and the natural world. As such, our lives should be devoted to the love of God and charity to all people. This way of life is founded on the practice of a variety of virtues, such as humility, forgiveness, moderation, generosity, gratitude, contentment, and patience. Further, we need to anticipate suffering and always remember that God suffers with us. So it is that suffering love is at the heart of life. At the same time, we need to acknowledge the presence of evil, but deny that it is from God.

We need to have few expectations and limit our desires. We need to understand that sickness and death are not from God. God's will is for wholeness and health, for fullness of life, and life with God forever. Taylor advises us to pray daily, to fast weekly, to keep the Sabbath, to worship regularly in the church each Sunday and on all holy days, to study and meditate on scripture, to tithe and give alms, to make a regular confession and seek spiritual guidance, and to use our time wisely in discerning and doing the will of God.

However, living such a life is problematic. We have been raised in a society that is convinced that there must be a cure for every disease. We dream about, long for, and are dedicated to finding such a cure. Therefore, when faced with a disease for which there is no known cure, our faith is tested if not shattered. Nevertheless, in spite of all our knowledge and skill, we and all our friends and loved ones will die, many before we believe they should. We know this, and yet we still ask, "Why?" and "Where is God?"

God did not create us because God was lonely and wanted our love. God created us because God needed to be able to share God's love, an unconditional, unmerited, and unending love, with creation. God is love and we are the subject of God's love. God's greatest desire is for us to be united in love. Because that is so, God had to create us with the freedom to reject God's love.

Further, God has an active and a permissive will. God does not will evil, sin, and death, but God permits them for a greater good. And that good is founded in God's desire and hope that we will choose to live with God in an ever-deepening relationship of love, a relationship that will last for eternity; a relationship for Episcopalians grounded in the example given to us by Jesus Christ.

There are a host of understandings about what comes after death. The traditional teaching of the church focuses on the resurrection of the body. It is an affirmation of faith founded on an amazing conviction, namely, that the human soul, understood as a material body, mind, and spirit, is destined to die, but has the capacity to be reborn with a new, nonmaterial body, mind, and spirit. While our descriptions of this state are metaphorical, they all point to the experience of being one with God, which is the meaning and purpose of our lives. It is a condition that is never static and is both personal and communal. Further, it is a gift that cannot be earned, but one offered freely to all who will accept it.

The church has always seen a foreshadowing of our end in our baptismal beginning. Baptism is our tomb, but it is also our womb. At our baptism, we experienced dying to sin, our separation from

God, and God's love. Immersed in baptismal water, we were drowned. We lost our breath and experienced death. There was nothing we could do to save our lives. We have to let go of life and our desire to control and manage life so that God can breathe new life, real life with God forever, into us.

At our baptism, the community of the baptized prays: "Thank you Father for the water of Baptism. In it we were buried with Christ in his death. By it we share in his resurrection. Through it we are reborn by the Holy Spirit." In Baptism, we have a foretaste of dying to all that enslaves us, dying to our old selves that we may be reborn. Our Christian hope at death is the same hope that sustains us throughout life, namely, that the God who has claimed us and loved us and held us in life will continue to do so in death. We believe this not because we believe in eternal life, but because we believe in the eternal love of God. We expect death from the beginning. Death is no surprise. It is that for which we spend our lives experiencing and preparing.

Our prayer book's burial services today are held in the context of an Easter Eucharist (pp. 491–505). The paschal candle, the resurrection music, and the sacramental meal in the reign of God proclaim and show God's love amidst death and commend the deceased to God's gracious mercy and peace. We have faith that, as in life, God's grace and love are our hope in death, not our good lives or our good deeds. Our trust and hope are not based on what we have done but upon our lifelong, daily experience of what God has done and is doing to make the experience of life, true and abundant life, possible now and forever. Eternal life is a surprising and graceful gift of a loving God who loves us in life and in death. Thus, resurrection is God's mighty act—and to it we witness.

How to live a holy life, a new life, a way of life made possible by our faith in the resurrection in the present is a testimony to our faith in Jesus' resurrection. There is no greater event in history than the faith of a small group of men and women in the resurrection of the historical Jesus. It turned the Jesus of history into the Christ of faith. And it both transformed those who had experienced this resurrection into a community of faith and sent them forth into a hostile world to risk and lose their lives on behalf of this strange experience. Amazingly, their proclamation of Christ's resurrection caught the imagination of the masses and became the distinguishing mark of a new religion, Christianity. On every Sunday, the first day of the week, these Christians gathered to celebrate the death and resurrection of the Messiah, the Christ, the anointed one who had ushered in the long-desired and hoped for reign of God. Mysteriously, God, through the death of Jesus, had destroyed the power of evil and redeemed the world. Life— true, abundant, and eternal life—was now the reality that ruled. Through Baptism, the experience of death and resurrection, persons were initiated into this new reality and empowered to live accordingly, that is, to abide in God's reign until it came in its fullness.

There is a creative, nurturing, and redemptive reality that overarches our lives, relieves our anxiety, and provides us with hope and the stimulus to live a holy life in the face of death. That brings us back to the first chapter about living into our baptism. God has made possible a new way of life for individuals and communities. In the mystery of death and rebirth, God has, through the life, death, and resurrection of Jesus, ushered in God's reign of justice and peace. Life in a domination-free, nonviolent, reconciled world, in which every human being receives all that he or she needs but no more, is as possible as life with God forever after death.

God has made possible a new way of life for individuals and communities. We can abide in God's reign now and forever. We can live, with God's help, a holy life, and by so doing, prepare for a holy death and rebirth to new life. And that is finally what it means to turn and follow Christ.

Notes

1 Carol Anderson with Peter Summers, *Knowing Jesus in Your Life* (Harrisburg, PA: Morehouse Publishing, 1993), 65–66.

2 Ibid., 73.

3 Daniel B. Stevick, *Baptismal Moments; Baptismal Meanings* (New York: Church Hymnal, 1987), 119, 137–38, 158.

4 Geoffrey Rowell, Kenneth Stevenson, and Rowan Williams, eds., *Love's Redeeming Work: The Anglican Quest for Holiness* (Oxford: Oxford University Press, 2001), xxvii.

5 Byron David Stuhlman, *The Initiatory Process in the Byzantine Tradition*, Gorgias Eastern Christian Studies 18 (Piscataway, NJ: Gorgias Press, 2009), 77.

6 Theodore of Mopsuestia, *Commentary on the Lord's Prayer, Baptism and the Eucharist*, chapter 3.

7 *The Rule of St. Benedict*, chapter 72.

8 Joan Chittister, OSB, *The Rule of Benedict: Insights from the Ages* (New York: Crossroad, 1992), 178.

9 Esther de Waal, *Every Earthly Blessing: Rediscovering the Celtic Tradition* (Harrisburg, PA: Morehouse Publishing, 1999), 14–15.

10 Margaret Guenther, *At Home in the World: A Rule of Life for the Rest of Us* (New York: Seabury Books, 2006), 11, 13.

11 See, for example, Margaret Guenther, *The Art of Spiritual Direction* (Cambridge, MA: Cowley Publications, 1992); Norvene Vest, ed., *Still Listening: New Horizons in Spiritual Direction* (Harrisburg: PA: Morehouse Publishing, 2000); and Alan Jones, *Exploring Spiritual Direction* (Cambridge, MA: Cowley Publications, 1999).

12 Rowell et al., *Love's Redeeming Work*, xix–xx.

Resources for Further Exploration

Anderson, Carol, with Peter Summers. *Knowing Jesus in Your Life.* Harrisburg, PA: Morehouse Publishing, 1993.

Black, Vicki K. *Welcome to Anglican Spiritual Traditions.* Harrisburg, PA: Morehouse Publishing, 2010.

Cottrell, Stephen, Steven Croft, Paula Gooder, Robert Atwell, and Sharon Ely Pearson. *Pilgrim: Turning to Christ.* New York: Church Publishing, 2016.

Curry, Michael B., and others. *Following the Way of Jesus.* Church's Teachings for a Changing World. New York: Church Publishing, 2017.

Gray-Reeves, Mary. *Unearthing My Religion: Real Talk about Real Faith.* Harrisburg, PA: Morehouse Publishing, 2013.

Guenther, Margaret. *Walking Home: From Eden to Emmaus.* Harrisburg, PA: Morehouse Publishing, 2011.

Law, Eric H. F., and Stephanie Spellers. *The Episcopal Way.* Church's Teachings for a Changing World. New York: Church Publishing, 2014.

Tammany, Klara. *Living Water: Baptism as a Way of Life.* New York: Church Publishing, 2002.

Wells, Samuel. *How Then Shall We Live? Christian Engagement with Contemporary Issues.* New York: Church Publishing, 2017.

Westerhoff, John H. *Living as a Prayer Book People.* Harrisburg, PA: Morehouse Publishing, 2004.

TURN: Pause, listen, and choose to follow Jesus

As Jesus was walking along, he saw Levi son of
Alphaeus sitting at the tax booth, and he said to
him, "Follow me." And he got up and followed him.
– Mark 2:14

"Do you turn to Jesus Christ . . . ?"
– Book of Common Prayer, 302

Like the disciples, we are called by Jesus to follow the Way
of Love. With God's help, we can turn from the powers of
sin, hatred, fear, injustice, and oppression toward the
way of truth, love, hope, justice, and freedom. In turning,

THE WAY OF LOVE

we reorient our lives to Jesus Christ, falling in love again, again, and again.

For Reflection and Discernment

- What practices help you to turn again and again to Jesus and the Way of Love?
- How will (or do) you incorporate these practices into your rhythm of life?
- Who will be your companion as you turn toward Jesus?

LEARN: Reflect on Scripture each day, especially on Jesus's life and teachings.

"Those who love me will keep my word, and my Father will love them,
and we will come to them and make our home with them." – John 14:23

Grant us so to hear [the Holy Scriptures], read, mark, learn, and inwardly
digest them. – Book of Common Prayer, 236

By reading and reflecting on Scripture, especially the life and teachings of
Jesus, we draw near to God, and God's word dwells in us. When we open our
minds and hearts to Scripture, we learn to see God's story and God's activity
in everyday life.

For Reflection and Discernment

- What ways of reflecting on Scripture are most life-giving for you?
- When will you set aside time to read and reflect on Scripture in your day?
- With whom will you share in the commitment to read and reflect on Scripture?

PRAY: Dwell intentionally with God daily

*He was praying in a certain place, and after he had finished,
one of his disciples said to him, "Lord, teach us to pray,
as John taught his disciples." – Luke 11:1*

"Lord, hear our prayer." – Book of Common Prayer

Jesus teaches us to come before God with humble hearts, boldly offering our thanksgivings and concerns to God or simply listening for God's voice in our lives and in the world. Whether in thought, word, or deed, individually or corporately, when we pray we invite and dwell in God's loving presence.

For Reflection and Discernment

- What intentional prayer practices center you in God's presence, so you can hear, speak, or simply dwell with God?
- How will (or do) you incorporate intentional prayer into your daily life?
- With whom will you share in the commitment to pray?

WORSHIP: Gather in community weekly to thank, praise, and dwell with God

*When he was at the table with them, he took bread, blessed and broke it,
and gave it to them. Then their eyes were opened, and they recognized him.
– Luke 24:30-31*

*Celebrant: Lift up your hearts. People: We lift them to the Lord.
– Book of Common Prayer, 361*

When we worship, we gather with others before God. We hear the Good News of Jesus, give thanks, confess, and offer the brokenness of the world to God. As we break bread, our eyes are opened to the presence of Christ. By the power of the Holy Spirit, we are made one body, the body of Christ sent forth to live the Way of Love.

For Discernment and Reflection

- What communal worship practices move you to encounter God and knit you into the body of Christ?
- How will (or do) you commit to regularly worship?
- With whom will you share the commitment to worship this week?

BLESS: Share faith and unselfishly give and serve

"Freely you have received; freely give." – Matthew 10:8

Celebrant: Will you proclaim by word and example the Good News of God in Christ?
People: We will, with God's help. – Book of Common Prayer, 305

Jesus called his disciples to give, forgive, teach, and heal in his name. We are empowered by the Spirit to bless everyone we meet, practicing generosity and compassion and proclaiming the Good News of God in Christ with hopeful words and selfless actions. We can share our stories of blessing and invite others to the Way of Love.

For Discernment and Reflection

- What are the ways the Spirit is calling you to bless others?
- How will (or does) blessing others through sharing your resources, faith, and story become part of your daily life?
- Who will join you in committing to the practice of blessing others

GO: Cross boundaries, listen deeply, and live like Jesus

Jesus said to them, "Peace be with you. As the Father has sent me,
so I send you." – John 20:21

Send them into the world in witness to your love.
– Book of Common Prayer, 306

As Jesus went to the highways and byways, he sends us beyond our circles and comfort to witness to the love, justice, and truth of God with our lips and with our lives. We go to listen with humility and to join God in healing a hurting world. We go to become Beloved Community, a people reconciled in love with God and one another.

For Discernment and Reflection

- To what new places or communities is the Spirit sending you to witness to the love, justice, and truth of God?
- How will you build into your life a commitment to cross boundaries, listen carefully, and take part in healing and reconciling what is broken in this world?
- With whom will you share in the commitment to go forth as a reconciler and healer?

REST: Receive the gift of God's grace, peace, and restoration

Peace I leave with you; my peace I give you. I do not give to you
  as the world gives. Do not let your hearts be troubled
  and do not be afraid. – John 14:27

Blessed are you, O Lord . . . giving rest to the weary,
  renewing the strength of those who are spent.
  – *Book of Common Prayer, 113*

From the beginning of creation, god has established the sacred pattern of going and returning, labor and rest. Especially today, God invites us to dedicate time for restoration and wholeness—within our bodies, minds, and souls, and within our communities and institutions. By resting, we place our trust in God; the primary actor who brings all things to their fullness.

For Discernment and Reflection

- What practices restore your body, mind and soul?
- How will you observe rest and renewal on a regular basis?
- With whom will you commit to create and maintain a regular practice of rest?